SO YOU WANNA BE A
TEACHER?

Abeja Reina

Without **Him**, I'm certain I wouldn't have gotten this far…

Hello my fellow colleague! If you're excited about becoming a teacher, yet still concerned about what to expect once you actually get your classroom, then this book will be the most informative quick read you will ever experience! I'm here to give you the skinny on a few tricks of the trade that I have used over the years that have assisted me towards becoming an exceptional teacher! This manual is a self-help guide, intended to give first-year educators a "real talk" perspective of the embodiment of an effectively successful teacher. There are a million and one professions out there and you decided to teach! Brave soul you are, so I put together this quick read for less than 10 bucks to hopefully give you the honest, light hearted twist to 21st-century education! There is space in the back of the book for note taking. You ready? Let's do this!

So now that you've completed the collegiate expectation part—you've taken several classes, originated a variety of thought-provoking projects—you feel excited and nervous at the same time, but overall you're ready to show what you've learned and what you can do! Your anxiety mainly comes from those unknown factors associated with teaching and operating a classroom, and you're thinking, "They couldn't have possibly taught me **everything** I need to know?" And you're right; they didn't! There's still so much that must be learned obviously, but what trumps? What do I really need to know to make my classroom; more importantly my career, run champ?

Your classes will instruct you on the basics, like writing a lesson plan, standardized cores, ideal instructional settings yada yada yada, it's all jargon, textbook savvy, it's almost cute. Not one of your college courses, not even your student teaching experience, is going to prepare you enough for your first year, and every year thereafter, as a teacher. You'll graduate feeling book smart, get that first credential, get a teaching gig, and be left to figure out the rest on your own!

This book offers a bird's-eye view of the unspoken truths in education, what is expected of you, as well as tips my colleagues and I have used over the years that can assist you in becoming classic. My objective, simply put, is to give you some quick points of reference to keep you focused on the big picture, produce some positive results here and there, but mainly to assist in preventing a "burn out" in as short a read as possible. Now I could list a million and one internet search strategies you could use in your classroom to manage your subjects academics, 90% of which you can find online in as quick as typing your name, or I could just give you a first-hand view of what I figured out over the years—what worked and what didn't. I'll just lay out a few key bullets as straight forwardly as I can, from my experience, naturally. A wise educator once told me, "It's always best to pull from the wheel then to recreate one. Education is an age old system, with ideas galore; your creativity is important, but nothing new. Therefore, these key ideas are intended to give clarity regarding those hidden factors associated with the modern day educational institutions.

So You Wanna Be a Teacher?

I decided to become a teacher after an awesome two-year experience as an assistant in a Kindergarten class in North Jersey. If I knew then what I know now, I probably would have become a doctor after all; it's much easier. Those two years were about as sugar-coated as my 15+ years in education have ever been. I didn't recognize then, nor do I fully understand now, the political propaganda behind the bulk load of our educational system. Each learning institution has a mission; however, due to so many political measures beyond anyone's control, matters pertaining to best practice for all learners tend to be the first to fade into the background. The goal is educating tomorrow's leaders; however, the reality is kids get left behind, STRAIGHT UP! Educational institutions, like prisons, are service providers—making money keeps the doors open, priority will always be business first!

I wanted to work with the 'lil guys; they're so much fun. But here I was a driven, highly-qualified educator, graduated in '02 with my first Masters in K-5 at Old Dominion in Virginia, moved back to California, and could not get a decent job to save my life! My years of experience working with my field of learners and credentials earned were just not enough to be considered by most of the respectable suitor districts throughout the LA area. This growing epidemic of mixed matched school district curriculum, unevenly distributed funding, maxed out classrooms, and unprepared teaching staff is nothing new, and remains prevalent. Districts will easily lay off highly qualified beginner staff to avoid legalities in getting rid of underqualified ineffective tenured or merit staff, it gets messy, with unions engaging in power struggles over matters that seem to be set in concrete!

I was eventually hired to work for one, of a series of Non-Public Schools in my area. I was being paid a fraction of the starting teacher wage and benefits. I would often think to myself that if I were to ever get a job through a respectable district, I would need to get smarter about the system. So, I went back to school, got my second masters in Special Education; a much longer program to complete then other credentialed programs by the way, but I graduated from a notable college in the Los Angeles area 2nd in my class. I learned the book expectations of a Sp.Ed. Teacher, and thank God I had already been working in that field on an emergency permit, or otherwise what I was learning would have hardly been useful application for the setting and student body I would be dealing with! The majority of those really awesome strategies I gathered were pointless if I was not able to manage myself and my classroom according to the 21st century learner. Its sink or swim, and we're teachers; we don't believe in drowning. The employment turnaround ratio for educators and related staff in several urban school districts throughout the United States is at unprecedented rates. Plainly stated, we are not being "schooled" on the hard knocks of the educational system upon entering the field. Consistency is being kicked under the rug for many of these schools to suffice growing demands, and political sticky fingers. Truthfully, the kids and educators, the ones that the system was designed to service are the first to be sacrificed.

How was I going to deal with this reality punch year in and year out, when it seemed to only be getting worse? I often wondered why I would see those senior teachers looking so lethargic, clearly unmotivated about learning, while entry-level educators moved forward with this sense of naivety? What happened? The senior teachers didn't start off that way! Why do so many simply give up? Because teaching ain't easy!! All those good and bad images that we associate with education on the TV are far from the truth. The reality is, it's neither horribly corrupt like the media advertises or perfectly sound like the district portrays, its all of that in between, which is by far way more challenging.

I'm so glad my fellow newbies are excited to learn more on how to get in the game and stay strong. No time for fluff! Let's start off with some motivational vibes, shall we?

<u>We Need You!!</u>

I just want you to know that you're one of a kind, rarity in its purest form! You are truly a diamond in the rough, hand-picked by our maker to be a leader in a field that in recent times has lost its popularity. Education is often the scapegoat for pretty much everything that could possibly go wrong in this country, and naturally passes the blame onto da da da daaa, TEACHERS! Teachers typically get the short stick whether all their efforts, implementations, tricks, and plans fail or succeed; it seems to never be enough to repair the damage done by a previous teacher who might have done the complete opposite.

Becoming a teacher won't necessarily give you that dream mansion in the hills or a flock of Facebook followers, and God forbid you get caught in a weekend act that ends with a video…hey it happens, and the outcome for teachers is always serious business. Long nights grading papers, subliminally planning unique abstract lessons on weekends, and wearing the many hats in and out of the classroom are a few amongst the many responsibilities that we have. One might not see the compensation for it all…but you do! What you will gain is self-satisfaction unlike no other. You mold tomorrow's leaders, give them hope, aspiration, and encouragement to face opposition with theory! Your determination is in demand! If ever a field had a **shortage** of highly effective, genuinely dedicated to the cause leaders, education is just that!

Teachers are the last of the Mohicans, the catalyst of change in a crumbling society. To teach is to lead others with the knowledge towards making better choices for themselves and their families. Educators who genuinely desire giving tools for others to produce results are in DEMAND! Our kids need us; our country needs us! Our ability to strive while overcoming those not-so-hidden oppressions within our society shows that we were molded from a different kind of clay.

Come into your new classroom with an open mind, a strong belief that **each** student, no matter their socio-economic or intellectual background, is vital to the system as a whole, these kids will impact our future some way, somehow, PERIOD! Therefore, they require the same supports as their counterparts. Aim for the maximum in all that you attempt to model, your students will be inspired by your energy, and aim to please you once they are certain that your true desire is to service them with the tools that they will need to be the BEST in life!

Stray away from the in-house dramas, negative staff, or hostile tenures. If this means that you are eating lunch in your room alone, so be it; trust me, your light, by law, cannot stay bottled up forever. Your passion for knowledge alone manifests your growth as a professional barer of information; therefore, opportunities will always be made available to you. You are an artist by design of introducing thought, your canvas is their minds, and you paint the images that activate the curiosity necessary for further exploration. You are a dream weaver!! It should always be your final call on what you will or will not tolerate in YOUR classroom, even if that means you have to go elsewhere!

As a trendsetter you will assist and one day lead the correction of those irreproachable stereotypes, tear down the barriers that say knowledge is optional, and pave way for a new system to take form! **Don't ever stop trying to do what's right**! You're going to come across negligent representatives, and see wrongful acts daily…yes, DAILY! As long as it is not directly harming the safety or well-being of your students, or yourself, simply take mental notes. One day you will be able to sit on an advising committee, and then you can pull out those observed discrepancies and begin sharing ways to cultivate a new system! A system composed of unfinished projects that will include collaborative input from other educators alike yourself. Your starting objective is to instruct, model and replicate. You may in fact be the only functional example that comes close to normality in those kids lives, remain steadfast in your quest, refusing to go against the most righteous and intended mission of education, and you too can make a difference! That was refreshing!

<u>First Thing's First</u>

Okay, so teaching is probably one of the last fields left that, by law and social norm, attests towards doing what is right at all times, setting the example, making the mark! That's right. You're like a human superhero, flawless by nature, knowledgeable of all things past, present, future, yet human…yeah right! Teachers are to uphold to a standard that many collegiate studies within the Arts and Sciences have long abated. Both at a professional and personal level, teachers are to live like Saints, **never** engaging in acts that depict any lack of moral conduct, or at least not getting caught. Even on our personal time! Our field consists of many magical moments found in a bottomless pit of formality. You are to blame if something does not work, and maintain if it does. It becomes so easy to establish a laissez-faire rapport, especially when recognitions are overlooked to account for incumbency. Just stay in the "middle" where it's safe...

> "For what will it profit a man if he gains the whole world and forfeits his soul? Or what shall a man give in return for his soul?"
>
> -Matthew 16:26

As an aspiring teacher, you must take a moment to ask yourself a series of questions before you nose-dive into a career that has little to no mercy on poor judgment. Your ability to grasp the overall nature of education—the good, bad, and super ugly—is vital to your long-term existence as a mentor. You have to be of sound character and mind, know who you are, and what you truly want out of teaching. Anything superficial, temporary, or instant should lead you to re-evaluate exactly what you are about to commit to.

Some people should not become teachers!

Teaching can be a lot like skipping college to join the military straight after high school...there's nothing easy about that at all! However, so many young adults perceive it to be so. It seems to be the next best alternative to paying for college while receiving living allowances. The popular perception is that anybody with a head can do it, and you can't really mess up that bad...or can you!? Teaching is a lifelong commitment, not a temporary gig; it's a mindset. You must be willing to continue learning throughout your career—both professional and street wisdom. That's right, your students and co-workers will not have the same learning experiences that you've had; they are all going to each be a completely different puzzle that you must learn.

By taking the time to decide if education is the right fit, you will be doing yourself and the many **thousands** of students you will encounter over the years a major favor! We can all recall that one teacher in school who absolutely hated his/her job, walking into the class every day with a bad attitude. The truth of the matter is those teachers really did not like going to work every day. They didn't like being disrespected and unappreciated, working long days to help many who may not want to help themselves, for miniscule pay. Mostly they didn't like themselves for not thinking through what they were getting into, and were then forced to ride it out, or take up a whole new career altogether. So ask yourself if teaching is something that your heart is in, or do the summer breaks sound P.H.A.T (pretty hot and tempting). Maybe it might help to know that those summer breaks are usually unpaid! Hmmmmmm…

So what are some of these questions, I'm sure there's more, but here's a few to get you started:

1. What type of Teacher do you want to be? (K-5, HS Math, Special Ed.)

2. Are you prepared to remain a lifetime learner with or without compensation?

3. Do you understand your responsibilities as an educator?

4. Are you capable of living a decent, upright life 24/7?

Okay so let's break down these top four questions real quick. Number 1, what type of teacher do you desire to become? If you did not already know this, it might be a bit of a shocker, but certain teaching positions are more difficult to obtain than others. Unfavorable and/or collegiately challenging positions in education are typically the most in demand, for example, single subject Math and Science and any and all areas of Special Education including added authorizations working with Autism and Reading are your more in demand positions. Meaning there are jobs available across the country, some may even give signing bonuses to get you to move. Ultimately they need your credential; they might be partially impressed by your teaching experience, and they may not. You could be the best Fine Arts teacher in the county; no one's fighting over you if the districts already have a fine art credential in position to satisfy the commission. Typically, there are those exceptions, and truly it's all about who you know, but hasn't it always been that way?

Now don't get me wrong, these are not bad fields. The added authorizations are more recent NCLB (No Child Left Behind) mandates; it's new, so your initiation to grow and learn a variety of strategies pretty much right along with your pupils is how you would master each. DO YOUR RESEARCH! Yes, you can be a 2nd grade music teacher; however, you and many others desire the one of few infrequently revolving positions needed, and music is slowly being cut from public schools across the U.S., which can also leave your credential partially obsolete. Be clear of specific hiring requirements and enroll in programs necessary to fulfill those requirements first, and then take add-ons later.

Number 2, are you prepared to become a lifetime learner? Even if the district or teaching commission doesn't ever come up with another mandated authorization to add to your teaching credential, which is highly unlikely, you are constantly being put to the test to assure that your instruction is generationally relevant to 21st-century educational expectations. Your students and colleagues will be your worst critics! They'll test your validity constantly, especially when they feel like they know more about topics then you do!

Be wise to stay informed; a teacher can risk losing his/her entire class to one over achieving student with a disruptive agenda. By staying two steps ahead of the game, you are more capable of brainstorming resolutions, even preventing everyday instructional delays and distractions. You are an educator, the world keeps going round, things change, and you have to stay up to date. There just isn't any time for excuses not to.

Number 3, do you understand your responsibilities as a teacher? As you explore the field of education, you will notice that there are many shaded areas of grey with regards to what is expected of you in the classroom. During your first year of teaching, you will embark on a journey of pure excitement—pinch me; I'm in charge of this class and everything in it! You're generally free to instruct as you see fit, as long as your lessons are within the common core realm of the content you specialize in. You'll aim to follow every rule and rarely question or confront authority. Keep in mind that education is a business. One rule may contradict another, while some may seem altogether irrelevant towards accomplishing the greater mission! As a first-year teacher, this is not your priority right now. Follow compliancy protocols as mandated and remain observational as you take note. No need complain or gossip about these matters; they're beyond your scope. Besides, it just builds a bad reputation for you.

Your job entails that you do your job alone, going above and beyond the call of duty is considered pro bono and up to your discretion. Anything less than expected could potentially cost you your position and more doesn't guarantee you'll keep it. Practice the art of moderation and discernment in all arising matters. Some things won't make an ounce of sense, so what can you do about it as a new teacher...absolutely nothing! Observe, take mental and written notation, even research possible resolutions, and wait. The perfect opportunity to assert your leadership skills in a public forum is in your future given your attention and obedience to detail as you grow.

apple You can ask your administrator specifics about your job duties, but who really has all the answers anyway! Remember, everyone has a job to do and your Administration's job is to follow protocol and keep up appearances. Administrators are typically Board selected through an annual evaluation for next term employment; therefore, most Administrators are hiring staff with the intention of building a team that is able to solve problems in a meaningfully collaborative effort without a whole lot of hand holding. Your growth in this field is determined by how many "likes" you get; however, your ability to stand strong throughout the years is based on how many tools you have gathered in your professional tool belt. So what is the best alternative to solve a given problem? What are the school district's mandates? What's considered appropriate classroom conduct at your site? Who can I ask if my admin is not directly available? This is a trial-and-error process that requires a consistent initiative of gathering and implementing resources, tossing out the ones that did not work, while searching for more, gaining collaborative colleague/admin support, and most importantly justifiable documentation that maps potential resolutions. One grain of sand at a time, you are becoming more effective at doing your job, and without even knowing it slowly introducing ideas of change into the system.

Hope you're still on board...Yeah I think you're a trooper; after all, you've read this far. This next one can be kinda tricky!

Okay Number 4, are you capable of living a decent, upright life 24/7? You are a leader, even if you do not directly see yourself as being so. Your choices in and out of the classroom shape the image that others will see of you. Even more so outside of work, you will be expected to adhere to a series of unmentioned guidelines. You will gain your stripes by other professionals in the field based off of your presentation, most often out of the classroom. Remember very few people will actually step foot into your classroom and watch you in action. Therefore, the only measure that can use to determine your work ethic is by how you present yourself on a regular basis outside of the classroom. Teachers typically get a bad rap in the media because so few, in and out of the profession, actually know what it is that we individually do all day!

Curiosity and entertainment leads the media to paint images about educators that is so far from truth, and for monetary gain, we become the "bad teacher," sex deviants and pedophiles, unsatisfied adults that passed on their dream job to teach! Wow I wish my life was that exciting! Truth is, as a new teacher you have to earn your respect as a trusted educator by demonstrating the upmost of professionalism, consistently, **AT ALL TIMES!**

This is never easy; those paroled high school buddies, pot head relatives, and drunk to violent friends may have to be avoided to some extent. Many times you will feel alone amongst your friends who selected more consumer relation or labor career paths. They speak openly about an employer and problematic job situation—you shouldn't! They get into it with those that they service or their direct supervisors—I wouldn't! They engage in wrongful acts before and/or after work (belligerent drinking, physical altercations etc…). What can I say, don't get caught! Your credential(s) are always on the line! Your referrals for future employment opportunities WILL come from your previous Administrators. And they talk to one another, quite frankly, more often than you think! DUI's, domestic violence, and addictions seem minor on the grand scope of how the world turns, but to a teacher this could mean the end of your career!

Furthermore, if you are accident prone, absent minded with important matters, a social drinker, or even a social network fanatic, BEWARE! Yeah it's okay for the "Average Joe," but you are the epitome of all that is wholesome, and any indication that you will drop the torch raises red flags, and districts do not like red flags. It scares them; they would rather dispose of the flag than have it go from green to yellow, which could potentially mean a major law suit, and worst, media publication. It sucks; it's the life of a teacher, I wish I could sugar coat it! I mean politicians, doctors, lawyers, almost any profession of similar status can get away with it, it's almost socially "cool" when they get caught, but NOT TEACHERS! We have to constantly be aware of our surroundings, and represent a character of prestige, accountability, wisdom, and control.

Bottom Line

Okay, so here's another something that you probably already knew, but not really: Everyone is a teacher! You are not the only teacher in your classroom! From your mom's lessons on keeping your room clean, your Auntie Barbara's drunken escapades during Thanksgiving dinner, to that one over-achieving, brown-nosing co-worker. We learn from everything that we come in contact with—

the world around us, our immediate environment, and every image that we see and hear are our teachers! It teaches us the foods we like, our style, as deep as how to discern an individual's intent in our lives. Life's experiences fill our internal filing cabinets with memories of information to build upon wisdom.

Your students, their parents, the lunch lady, and janitorial staff are all teachers. Your students, by number, are the largest body of teachers on your school campus, for they impress upon one another with information upload faster than the adult teachers ever could, therefore they are the most influential. Therefore, as leaders, we must take into account what the students are teaching one another (the trends of the day).

Our ambitions in life, our interests, and beliefs vary based off of our perception of the world around us, and all the key characters within it. Once you're able to fully grasp the concept that there is no one way to learn ANYTHING, you will be comfortable with the notion that there is no one way to teach! So don't attempt to copy any one teaching method to the point. Your style, your charm, and glow are a individual set of gifts all your own, and it becomes that uniqueness that will mold you towards becoming an effective educator. That's all! No books, no resources alone are able to give you that cookie cutter, matter-of-fact plan on how to operate your classroom and its contents. Only application over time! There is no set mastery level, you just keep doing it!

So for decades, many great minds have come up with highly researched and tested formulas of classroom management. Some have worked, many have failed, and each classroom environment is COMPLETELY different from the next. So you ask yourself, "Which instructional method will actually work for me?" There is no answer to that question, folks; it's all information obtained through application done over time. In other words, you have to implement each strategy case by individual case. Through trial and error, collecting mental and written data, until you find the right fit, and even then things change. Your goal is to gather as much as you can, become as well-versed as you can, and be willing to continue learning more!

You might get a site change letter and re-locate schools or classrooms, as annual enrollment changes. You've designed lessons that are now supplemental to an outdated textbook or curriculum. The list goes on and on. Teachers are literally the miracle workers of knowledge. We have to know a little bit of everything, which takes time. With that being said, time is your best clue to becoming an effective teacher! Oddly enough, time is the one factor we have no control over and as little as possible of, GEESH! This is why I encourage you not to jump ship prematurely. If you truly desire to become an effective educator, you will need to gather a variety of formulas on the "to do's" and "not to do's" of operating a productive learning environment with varied learners. So start a digital scrapbook of ideas, and collecting a slew of artifacts, borrow from your co-workers and be willing to share, don't re-invent the wheel, it's going to be a lifetime journey!

#1 Be Willing to Stay for the Long Haul

<u>Personality Type</u>

If entertaining is not your personality type, paaallleeezzz reconsider your profession choice! A funny job requirement for teachers should entail that we can perform magic tricks! Yup, that's because putting on a well enacted performance is honestly what you will have to do to produce results. We know the literal lesson plan, the district's curriculum guide, but our kids don't, actually most could care less! How are we to interpret a boring set of objectives, goals, and yada yada yada to a group of learners who really just wanna have fun? So we have to make learning fun! You may not have to sing or dance in front of your kids, but you will have to dazzle them, otherwise no matter how awesome your lesson is, not one student will remember one thing taught! Even with enthusiasm they still may not remember anything, but the probability is higher with than without. The goal is to get them to retain enough to move forward, you have a time line to adhere to, and a continual flow of students to prepare for the next level.

This concept has a fine line; some will read this and take the idea to a whole other level that could possibly cost them their job. Others will rationally break it down, and put in a dab here and there, appearing almost phony (kids can detect things like that by the way).

The ones who get it will establish a learning environment that "keeps it real." This teacher will give positive, articulated instruction, supplemented with generational relevant technology, engage learners in appropriate whole class discussion, while scaffolding supports with flare, linking "did you know?" concepts for learning across the curriculum and real world, frequently checking for understanding. This educator will go the extra mile to ensure that they provide a rigor that is challenging, informative, yet meaningful to each learner's life.

So set the mode in your classroom to assert the type of learning that is to take place at given times. Not every lesson has to be given the same way. SURPRISE them! Change it up! Do it outside! Let them see another way to learn the same material through visuals, hands-on projects, and community-based field trip opportunities; the material will stick longer the more out of the box you design and instruct the lesson.

#2 Be Creatively Energetic

<u>Know Your Kids</u>

As teachers, we must remain cognitively aware that we are also learners, and we have to be willing to actively learn to continue to teach. Ideally, to best instruct a group of learners, it is important that we are in tune with each pupil and how they themselves learn. This is not always easy to do, and there is no exam or measurement to tally mark off whether or not you have done this right. However, the more effort you place on getting to know your students will show in your overall classroom instruction and management.

In other words, people will know if you know! So this may not cost you your job, but we all can recall those teachers in school that everyone respected and raced to take a class with vs. the teacher no one wanted. The question we have to ask ourselves is: do I desire to become an effective educator, or simply get by to get paid? Taking the time to get to know individual learners will give you a leg up on behavioral management/prevention, requesting the most appropriate tools/resources for each learner, inevitably shaping a more productive classroom environment.

Some icebreaker questions you might want to ask yourself as you assess and collect mental and written data about your students.

- What are they interested in learning/favorite subjects (in and out of school)?

- What is their family background, as much as you can gather (place of birth, culture, language, current residence, family dynamics and affiliations)?

- Strengths/weaknesses, short/long-term goals, pet peeves, and antecedents?

- Minor to major learning disabilities (with or without an IEP)?

- Just see where their heads are!

The more you know, the more you know! Become familiar with your students as much as you can, and give them a reason to trust your empathetic advice. They WILL respect your professional position in the classroom, and also the validity of the information that you are teaching them once they know that you care for and respect them individually.

#3 Be Willing to Know and Learn your Kids

<u>Classroom Management</u>

Organization & Structure

This is one of my favorite topics on effective teaching. I am a strict organizer; I do not do well with clutter at all! Therefore, one would think that this arena of classroom management works wonders for me; but that is not necessarily true. I have to remind myself to be logical. If the students are actively engaged in a messy or loud project, I have to force myself to be flexible in my borderline OCD approach to classroom organization.

If you are on either end of the spectrum of organization, you will need to prioritize your habits, and set goals to fix them! So for example, if you find yourself in a constant frenzy—papers and wrappers galore—then a timed organizational goal is in order; start at home and begin your year with having a set place to put stuff. Establish one small goal; add one more smaller goal to make a medium sized goal and so on so forth. If you are easily rattled by imperfections of the classroom environment, often rigid in your management, you have to be realistic. A wise administrator once told me that she never wants to walk into an immaculate grade school classroom, because that means the kids weren't learning. Each learning environment should be organized conducive to that classrooms subject, avoid being overly rigid, yet plan to adhere to a working structure that can logically yield the results of an intended lesson.

Students are able to further grasp concepts associated with organization through a first-hand account as to how managed their teacher(s) are. Does the teacher have a hard time locating important stuff? Does the class itself start on time? Is the classroom a complete mess? Is it too hot or too cold inside the room? Has the teacher established precedence on neatness, timeliness, and effort? Organization is the key to effective instruction!

Now somebody out there is going to counter this notion by saying, "I know my mess and where everything is…" Well I'm here to tell you that the remaining 99.9% of the rest of us don't (remember perception is key). Your students will behave according to the temperature in the classroom, figuratively and literally speaking! If the teacher is always on the cliffs edge with assignments, lectures, even where he/she sat down their personals, the students will respond accordingly! They too will display irregularities in their ability to effectively organize their assignments, schedules, even to separate what is appropriately expected of them in your classroom (i.e., leaving trash on the floor, gum chewing in class, assignment completion, and submission).

Kids and adults alike have an uncanny ability to discern the "easy" people from the "hard" people, just based on one's ability to manage their environment. They will respect your commands, and take serious your requests when they see your "house in order." Why?? Because they unconsciously recognize that you have very few flaws in your program, so few that they see it being more work to argue your expectations, than just doing them. They cannot easily break your management, and in trying could potentially risk undesirable consequences, so they learn to avoid it all together! REAL TALK! Your students are your pack, and you are the alpha. They will follow your lead, even if it is wrong, up until they feel that your position can be over thrown. In knowing this, you will never need to raise your voice, lose your composure, or give incentives to earn respect, because your **presentation** (organization) alone demands it!

On the contrary, if your classroom management has no flexibility, displays a lack of empathy regarding others' organizational habits, or simply feels like a military lineup, you will lose some of your students. They will stray, and not because your management is impossible for them to keep up with, rather because they recognize your emphasis on yourself rather than them. Be willing to compromise and make the classroom just as much theirs as your own by working with some of their habits. They would rather defy you, disrespect you, even so far as attempt to catch you "slipping" than follow your dictatorship. Be realistic and flexible in your organization.

#4 Get Realistically Organized!

You are not their friend! Yet you show them through modeling how to maintain appropriate relationships with one another (needed for being in the work place), how to organize their affairs (needed for adult independency), and most importantly, how to follow directions (needed to SURVIVE IN LIFE!). Your ability to manage their learning environment can make or break their ability to learn and retain, as well as your ability to do your job effectively!

I hope some of this is making sense to you, following directions is key to our profession; we don't have to remake the wheel if it works. Through setting small personal goals and applying them, any individual desiring to do so can manage their work environment each and every time! So don't give up!

Discipline Control

Whether you teach an Emotional Disturbed SDC class or a General Ed. Honors Trig course, you WILL always come across some form of misbehavior that may require disciplinary measure. As I stated earlier, your students figure out early on when a teacher is "weak," or incapable of managing their class. Human beings are more innate to follow a leader who displays the traits of being strong enough to lead.

Many times students' disciplinary concerns develop from outside factors that have nothing to do with you and your performance; however, it is your responsibility to manage these behaviors on all levels.

Minor Disruptions

Students who engage in minor in class disruptions are either academically confused or are seeking attention, one usually leads to the other. If a student is completely engaged in an assignment, whether they will get a high grade or not, they are often engaged in more than the lesson. Your lesson has activated their curiosity, calling for them to know and/or do more. Very rarely does a young learner (K-12), or an adult for that matter, intentionally set out to learn about a subject that they have no interest in. Therefore, minor disruptions, no matter a student's disability or not, can be controlled with a consistent flow of incentive or reprimand, along with a variety of engaging time configured lessons.

Incentives are your small, "caught being good" tokens for positive pupils, and "you missed out, maybe next time" for disruptive ones. Examples include verbal praise, "good job on that assignment, high five," end of class breaks, no more than 5 minutes, low-cost knick knacks, and goodies. Your incentives are used to control minor disruptions and intended to be given as a positive reinforcement to

28

those students doing what is expected of them without reminders. Change up how you measure when a student or even group of students has earned an incentive, and don't share the measurement scale with them; that away they never truly know whether their behavior is being observed or not, so to always remain appropriate.

Reprimands are consequences for an undesirable behavior. Having already given the student verbal warnings, a reprimand should be issued (lost recess/lunch time, lowered assignment points earned, or a note/call home) each and every time a minor disruption has taken place. They key to reprimands more than incentives, is CONSISTENCY! The level of one reprimand issued needs to equal to the level of another reprimand issued for similar behaviors. This consequence must be set in stone, no matter the student or time of day (in school). This establishes your genuinely fair attitude that you will maintain with your pupils, and they will notice this! Be consistent with your reprimands!

As Alpha of your classroom, your pack (the other attentive learners) depends on your ability to control and prevent disruptive situations. Disruptions make your class as a whole feel tense, nervous, unprotected, and unsure about your ability to manage their environment. Those students that display an inability to control themselves in class must be used as whole class examples, so don't ever forget to follow through with the reprimand. Use disruptive students as an example of what you **will not tolerate** in your classroom!

This is in everyone's best interest that you shake your mane and let them see who the leader of the classroom truly is. It can be done discretely at first, until you have learned the temperaments of your learners, and then you can adjust the level of each example setting session you orchestrate. I usually like to incorporate an observed negative behavior during my lesson; it hits two birds with one stone.

EXAMPLE

Today's Lesson: English: Grammatical structure

"Awoke and awake are different usages of the same word; one is present the other is past tense, meaning it's happening or it already happened. For example, our classmate Joey here, well he must have been awoke til 2am in the morning which is why he is so sleepy in my class today vs. When Joey is awake he will be able to take great notes for the exam tomorrow!"

If Joey is one of your students struggling with the overly used behavior of sleeping in class, you are asserting to Joey, and the rest of the class, that you are well aware of the unacceptable behavior; they could get called out for displaying this inappropriate behavior, as well as potential consequences. Others, who might have felt brave enough to disrupt your class, or engage in a similar behavior, will learn hopefully from that, including many other timely distributed examples you have made, and choose not to negatively partake.

You can lessen and even eliminate minor disruptions by always engaging students in time-managed, meaningful instruction. Students who are bored typically find "down" time to seek attention—Laughs here or there, small conversations amongst learners, shouting out answers. Do not lose your cool over these occasional immaturities; rather, choose to redirect the student with a number of fair verbal warnings. There is no set number of verbal reprimands, because it's based on each learner. But trust me, you will know when a child is taking advantage. If the behavior continues, a written contract with the student's and parents' signatures containing more extensive reprimands are in order, as well as re-evaluating the students' weaknesses regarding the subject matter (they may require additional supports or non-IEP teacher made modifications such seat reassignment, ignoring). If the behavior continues, you the classroom leader must take noticeable action each and every time to eradicate the behavior all together.

Note that these are simply examples; I understand each student and setting are completely different from the next, so you have to shape an incentive/reprimand system that works for you. Another suggestion is to always have your lessons ready to go once that bell rings. Give the students little to no time to find mischief. Keep them engaged the duration of the period, either through lecture, independent work, or brain games (puzzles, word search, and online fundamentals practice).

Always maintain a collection of spare mini-activities to use if the lesson runs short, or you notice that your students have completed their assignment early. Some listed suggestions below have helped me tremendously in those rare occasions, because typically you'll need more time, more than not having enough. You can also incorporate these ideas in your lesson and link them to previously taught curriculum. A little research and development goes a long way, the students won't know they finished early (haha), and you will have kept them engaged in a productive learning experience until the next class.

1. Brain games & optical illusions

2. Fascinating "Did you know?" facts about popular people, places, things, animals etc…

3. Riddles & brain teasers

4. Timed cross word puzzles, mazes, word searches

5. Extra credit/make-up work opportunities

Major Incidents

Based on the dynamic of your school and classroom setting, you may experience verbal threats or physical confrontations in your classroom. Clearly, no teacher desires to break up a fight; however, on those occasions you will need to respond both to the incident in a safe and professional manner. Remember, in most cases your students' disciplinary problems will have nothing to do with you. Outside factors that have stemmed over from lunch, home or after

32

school are the most common culprits. In my line of work, I've come to conclude that in many cases, students also know whose classroom would be the best fit to engage in these types of altercations. Don't let your classroom be one of them! Once again they are looking for the weakest link, so you set the precedent on what you will accept in your classroom from day 1!

If a major incident takes place in your classroom, your goal is to dismantle the tussle before it starts. In most cases, aside from Court School (Juvie) or Camps, words come before fists. If you are able to calmly disengage a verbal confrontation between two students, or de-escalate one over the top pupil, DO SO! However, in the case that a physical altercation happens in your room, your main goal is to protect:

1. Your other students

2. The fighting student(s)

3. Then yourself

Yep, all in that order! Clear the non-aggressive learners as far away from the fight as possible, and call for assistance from the office (security or behavior management support staff). Based on your school site, a training on physical restraint may be given to you, especially if that is the type of environment that you're working in, however if not,

DO NOT TOUCH THE STUDENTS!

One might argue this matter of fact, but I'm here to tell you that during a fight, it is so easy to take your room and its possessions as a personal attack against you. Your intention is to stop the fight, avoid anyone or anything from getting hurt or destroyed, but your emotions are saying, "How dare you fight in my classroom!" You might have an initial response to do so, but once 'hands on' a student (client) has been established, it becomes your word against theirs and that is always risky business. Move the non-aggressive students out of the way and call the office for security. If this type of behavior is happening frequently, inform your direct supervisor that you may need training on how to handle physically aggressive student(s).

You will be responsible for writing an incident report of the on goings before, during, and after the altercation. Clearly eye witness testimonies from other staff and students can support your interpretation of the events that led up to the fight. Be mindful that not everyone will give the correct interpretation of events, so to avoid being accused of anything inappropriate, before you decide that you are going to put hands on the aggressive student(s), demand that another staff member assist you.

Unless otherwise directed as a part of your job responsibilities, it is your personal discretion to establish any type of physical contact with your students (i.e., side hugs, high fives, shoulder pat, separating a fight, or de-escalated learner). Teachers often purchase work hazard insurance in the case of a legal action taken, however this does not avoid a teacher's employment file from being tarnished. It is in the

34

best interest of the credentialed teacher to not ever touch their student(s) during a physical confrontation unless having been properly trained to do so. Like an independent contractor, it's your responsibility to know what the right thing to do is, and if you are not trained, you just don't know, and if you respond it's your career/credential on the line, because the situation is very very fine-lined!

I have worked in some of the most hostile environments in my 15 years of teaching Special Education. From locked psychiatric units to inner city Juvenile Halls, I've seen it all from the behavioral aspect from an educational stand point. In these environments, a high level of tension exists among the pupils and staff and instruction quality is a challenge, because behavior incidents are so frequent. Clearly classroom management is the key to maintenance within these types of settings; however there are times when a confrontation is pre-planned and cannot be de-escalated. Student and teacher safety are always top priority. You are an instructor, not a ring leader. You commit to doing the best you can to protect the students, and yourself! Going above and beyond the call of duty could cost you your job, work smarter not harder!

#5 Address Negative Behaviors and be Consistent!

Settings & Modifications

Your classroom itself is a visual aid to support the curriculum you are teaching, and should reflect so by displaying an array of wall arrangements that should motivate and promote assistance towards learning that subject matter. Although, many students in a general education classroom do not have IEP's, you as a 21st century instructor will need to be diverse and flexible in your teaching style to service a variety of learners, including special and exceptional needs students.

Keeping the classroom temperature at a comfortable 72-75 degrees works well for the majority of folks; however, for those unique cases, you can make seating accommodations, purchase supplements (revolving fans and allowable space heaters) or put in a regular flow of justifiable work orders until the problem is remedied. After a familiar assessment of your pupils, you will be able to enact management techniques that assist students in making better choices without having to stop instruction.

EXAMPLE

*Students who tend to 'run their own program' (**not diagnosed Sp.Ed**) should be placed in the front row; a suggestive tip is to keep the classroom doors open, no bars up, sending the message that this is **their** education, ultimately **their** life choices. By doing so you are allowing all of your students the opportunity to make positive mature choices regarding their own behavior in class. Knowing that there are consequences, most of your students will comply with the rules to avoid adverse commentary or sheer embarrassment. This technique is ideal for students who struggle with impulsivities, yet aim to display themselves acceptable towards their teachers and peers. By placing*

36

them in the front row, their actions are immediately noticed, and can be called out. Peer approval is a much more monumental feat, and over time, the student will see that his/her behavior has no impact on anyone but self, and hopefully, he/she will decide to make better choices.

Place all of your visual wall aides at a level appropriate to their function, and keep student work samples updated with positive, constructive comments. Always have active work on your board, and only erase the work once you've replaced it with more work, or if additional board space is needed. You are shaping the minds of your students to always be actively engaged; therefore, you should be as well. Avoid distractions involving your cell phone—yes, I know how hard this is! Fraternizing with aides or other teachers for extended periods of time, or having a "small chat" with your students (they too can be guilty of pulling you along), all shorten instruction time. The phrase, "there is a time and place…" is exactly how you have to visualize the ongoing instruction in your classroom. Students and staff will love to share odd tales here and there and distractions will happen, keep it task related and focused on the intended lesson as much as possible, or an entire period can be easily wasted.

Pre-establishing a sufficient instruction plan, in a comfortably safe setting makes your class time fly by! Leave them feeling confident about what they just learned, end on a light note with a strong reiterating fact, and on to the next lesson. Your students appreciate your patience; they admire your determination to remain consistent and organized. You're in control of your working environment, so the majority of the pressure can focus on instruction, because all other factors are managed! Now, do it again, and again, each day, with aspiring motivation coming from timed creativity, just like sharpening a tool or aging a fine wine.

<u>Time to Teach</u>

Lessons

Most districts have established curriculum that coincides with a set of pre-selected state standards (these are learning objectives for each subject). As a new teacher, you will be supplied with the generalized idea of what you are expected to instruct; the actual lesson planning, assessments, grading, and implementation are all up to you. The key to this is CREATIVITY! The more interesting and creative a lesson is, the more the kids will participate and recall. A simple lesson, for example, is to read a passage of text and answer questions; generally speaking, that is all that is expected of you; however the lesson planning is the part where your inner born to lead dendrites can fire off! Therefore, get carried away! The more flare the better! If you struggle with this idea, a career revaluation is in order. This is the best part to being a teacher, so you'd have to ask yourself why wouldn't you want to give it your all?

The issue of time will always be a vice, and is typically the main culprit behind an unsuccessful lesson; you can't win them all! So set time lines on high-end assignments, these are lessons that force you to use Bloom's Taxonomy (Google it if you don't know) vs. traditional assignments involving a read and end of chapter answers session or supplemental worksheet. Try everything at least once; you'd be surprised what works well for one group of learners may not hit it off with another, so keep testing the water and commit to lessons that may take longer, yet always tend to be a big hit!

Your lessons should be designed to intrigue your pupils so much that they yearn to further investigate, not have them dozing off. You are going to have those occasional nodding heads during class (there's always 1 or 2); however, as a whole, most of your class should be engaged, if just by your enthusiasm alone. Learners that are being academically challenged will always have a task in front of them, they understand how you run your program, and are eager to engage and show you how much they've learned. Eventually, that one non-compliant student will follow suit, or fall off, which in both cases none of the other students are greatly affected.

apple   I know this may seem harsh, but the truth is, to sacrifice one for the greater good is a choice that every leader will have to decide upon in their career. Your job is to give your all to each and every learner, then all you can do is sit back and pray for survivors. As I have stated earlier, in most cases, matters beyond your control can and will affect the temperament of your student(s). It's beyond anything that you can do, and you're not expected to save the world that way anyway. You job is to model what is appropriately expected of you as a teacher and leader in order to reach as many learners as you can in a very short duration of time before they enter into adulthood. Maybe another teacher out there will be the life-changing mentor for that one student that you just couldn't seem to reach. So it's not the end of the world! If you are genuinely doing your part, then mission accomplished! In the end you are your only accountability!

As mentioned earlier, you yourself are also a continuous learner. If there is a subject that you do not know enough about, it is your professional obligation to take the time and "school" yourself! All that you gather can be brought into your classroom in some shape, form, or fashion. If it's a word and you say it more than 23 times non-consecutively, you'll never forget it! Amazing how the brain works and yours is an all-encompassing search engine. The more you know, the more your students will learn!

#6 A Lesson Planned is a Lesson Learned

Your next responsibility as a leader is to critically assess the areas within your instruction methods that display struggle, think about what you could do differently the next time in you're planning, gathering and presentation. As time goes on, you will develop a knack for lesson planning, having gathered some really great ideas over the years, as well as establishing a presentation technique that works for you!

Ideally, you have standards to adhere to, so you have a general template of what your lessons will encompass; now add the accessories. Change'em up and seek suggestions from other more experienced teachers. Be tech savvy and incorporate technology as much as possible; stray away from thinking that every assignment must accompany a pencil and paper. Be willing to assess your students with verbal responses, or by having them co-teach the class. You can also solicit the support of your teacher's assistants or aides to "co-teach" and participate in planning on a subject that they may have personal experience in.

Here's some do's and don'ts that have worked for me over the years:

Do's

- Plan your lessons around the standard or topic given to you to teach, be willing to change how you dissect (modify) and execute the lesson.

- BE CREATIVE with your presentation!

- Use other teacher's ideas, steal them all you want!

- Collaboration with your colleagues is GOLD!

- Ask questions/do your research on content that you are not clear about.

- Prepare your lessons in advance! Toughie! I know, recall strong (project or community based) vs. traditional (end of chapter questions or worksheet) assignments.

- Follow the traditional lesson plan break down to ensure that your learners are getting a variety of pieces to the generalized lesson idea (Anticipatory Set, Objective, Guided Instruction, Independent Practice, Closure).

- Allow the students to "co-teach" the class; this is fun and informative for them

- It's okay to make mistakes while you're teaching; if they notice, let them correct you. Show that you are human, and even as an adult, remain a lifetime learner

- Not everything you teach will stick, the more variety in your instruction, the better the information is stored for recollection

Don'ts

- Turn to video instruction as a 'save all' lesson, only as a supplemental resource to the lesson.

- Throw student work away, keep a filing cabinet, every little bit shows progress, and give it back to them or show their parents quarterly!

- Make stuff up to compensate; let them watch you teach yourself, go online in front of them and do a mini research to confirm validity of your instruction.

- Fail a student because you don't like them. This has happened more often than we know, and on the reverse side has negatively impacted the teacher. Keep more than a grade book; have a system inline that students and parents know how you assess assignments, along with frequent reminders for failing students

Data Collection

Keeping a written/typed log of your classrooms is the most helpful tool that a teacher has if any allegation is ever made. An anecdote is a quick written description of a situation, any situation, good or bad. Concise, organized, anecdotes show administrators, parents, and students how serious you are about the goings-on in your classroom. Data collection is a team effort; therefore your aides (if you have any) can help gather this information as well because more eyes give a clearer picture. Collecting data displays noticeable evident of a professional working environment.

Keep records of goals set, by setting in classroom goals for each learner to improve upon your giving the student an opportunity to correct and replace a negative trait with a positive one. Keep written documentation of positive and negative student work ethics, work ability, and attitude. Students will be surprised by the short, straight to the point data collected on them; have a simple rubric of measures that they can improve upon and build confidence with the positive notes taken about them. Regularly remind your aides and class as a whole that certain behaviors will be written down even if you become too busy and forget to do so, they are now aware that they are being observed and will feel more accountable for their actions (rewards vs. reprimands).

#7 Document, Document, Document!

One of the more challenging aspects of our job as visionaries is handling matters involving parents. Let's face it, these kids nowadays are a handful, Sp. Ed. or not, and I can assure you that the apple never falls far from the tree. The 21st-century parent works, meaning less time to discipline, go over homework, and become that fundamental component to their developing learner. There are different types of parents; you will gather the most insight on a child's parent as you get to know your students. I make an effort to initiate a routine parental contact either via phone, email, or even text. In doing so, you will have established a safe ground with them so that the feel comfortable talking with you when urgent matters arise. Remember, their child is your client (your job), so tone, word selection, and overall attitude can easily make or break ongoing communication with parents, and you want ongoing communication to exist. Parents should be encouraged to call if they have a concern, and work with you as their child's teacher, while building a partnership to remedy matters and support their learner's educational goals.

More often than not, your parents are going to place the bulk load of educating their child in your hands; slowly place some of that responsibility back in their hands. Remind parents frequently what their job entails as a parent in working with their learner. Support parents with a variety of useful tools in solving various academic and/or behavioral concerns, and encourage them to further expand upon the lessons taught with their student during non-school time. Your students' parents are going to see something in their child that you may not see; there is no need to ever argue that. Simply do the best at your job to provide an appropriate education to their child, reminding parents of their role as an advocate in the overall picture within their child's educational progress.

Avoid any and all 1:1 confrontations with hostile parents. As educators, we must always protect ourselves from hidden agendas; therefore, I would encourage all teachers to avoid being alone in a meeting with an irate parent or student. Always have a least one additional staff or admin present and able to attest to the 1:1 conversation taking place. Teachers are responsible for defending their professional decisions regarding students in their classroom; realistically, the only way to do this is to keep a written anecdotal record of the student throughout the day and all conversations with a parent and/or student. Have a designated folder, put the date, with whom, and jot down a brief summary of words exchanged. Remember it is always your word against theirs, even if they were wrong, you are the easier target. **ALWAYS PROTECT YOURSELF!**

Resources

The best part about being a teacher, aside from the summer and holidays off, is your freedom of instructional expression and its academic effectiveness with your students. A collection of online and hard copy resources, tangible artifacts, search key words, and visuals will become the most beneficial to supplementing your lessons. Your ability to know how to operate a computer, email, internet searches, notebooks, and other educational technology (Smart board, Elmo, Projector) will make for an exciting teaching experience for your students as well as yourself.

The idea is to save everything, which lessens the amount of research gathering you will need to do for the next time. A flash drive should be the second thing on your key ring next to your filing cabinet and classroom key. That drive can hold folders containing self-generated tests, helpful search links, supplemental worksheets, and all saved lessons in Word so you can cut and paste, easily revise, update as needed, and share with colleagues.

Most books, although becoming obsolete in form, are typically adopted every 5-7 years or so; however, by the time you actually obtain the book, the information could be outdated. Therefore, the internet is your best source for most up-to-date info. Teachers that do not know or care to operate technology are doing their students a **TREMENDOUS** disservice! If you don't know how to operate them, you need to learn! Most districts provide in-service professional developments to train teachers on tech savvy skills, however it is your responsibility to know tech age basics if they do or do not offer this training. Your Admin will surely support you if you want to learn more, trust me; they want you to know how!

Administrators can be quite friendly with funding— sounds funny, right? Well if they have it, they want to spend it, or they'll lose it. Many Inc. LLC big business manufactures who desperately seek annual tax write off's will also be overly generous if solicited. Schools gather funding from set annual sources, and their allotment doesn't change much aside from influxes in enrollment, Sp. Ed. Law updates, or curriculum advancement program needs. Common Core and our new adopted system in California called Smarter Balance will require that all schools have a set number of network compatible computers, software, and training. So schools will get funding to compensate this new need. When Admins have additional monies, they can supply teachers with more specific requests, so long as the teacher shows a need. Most teachers become so overwhelmed with the abundance of trendy tech resources that they already have in their classrooms, yet have no idea on how to use them.

Ask your Admin if you can enroll in some tech support professional development on how to learn using all of the stuff collecting dust in the resource closet, it could greatly benefit you. You know the saying, "a closed mouth…" well this rule applies heavily in education. If you do not request something in your classroom, it is presumed that you already have an alternative formula that works just fine. Therefore, your mission is to always ask; even if it's farfetched, ASK! Chances are someone in your school may have advice or a potential resolution; either way you will be more better off than when you started if you put the word out.

#8 Ask, and You Shall Receive Resources

Tricks of the Trade

Off-Task Behavior

Frequent off-task behaviors such as sleeping, fumbling with electronics, and daydreaming are all common, reoccurring problems in every classroom. Recall that in most cases none of these behaviors are a personal attack on you as the leader in the room. You are responsible for wearing many hats; therefore, you should never exhaust yourself day in and out on those off-task students. In my years as an educator, I've seen that you can remedy most off-task behaviors by placing little to no attention on them, and focus on the students that are alert, focused, and want to learn.

I am a firm believer in the motto "silence is golden," and after building a positive rapport with my learners of the classroom rules and expectations, I practice this proverb in theory by slowly digressing my voice of authority in the classroom, allowing students to de-escalate their own tones, emotions, and attitude when talking with me over tense matters.

This low tone to silent treatment, accompanied with noticeable anecdotal notation in their files and small gestures, gives the student(s) time to reflect on what they already know about the expectations in my class and select the better behavior. This does not mean you are allowing your students to engage in a free for all, it

48

simply means that you, the voice of reason, becomes less aggressive and/or argumentative. Trust me, if you have reiterated the rule enough, they know it by heart. You are scaffolding positive behavior choices. In each given occurrence, I remind them once, maybe twice how the results of their actions will affect them, and I leave it alone…As long as the behavior is not distracting. I continue to instruct, marking my dominance in the room as the Alpha force, my body language and tone remain un-phased, and I'll be sure to praise (small incentive) those students who remain on task, using them as example figures of what is expected of them in my classroom.

I've gotten so good at this technique that I am able to intertwine the idea into any lesson while I am teaching my content. Every lesson has a moral, and especially so if I have a defiant learner. Refuse to change your spirit, tone, and attitude, while you continue to offer that student the opportunity to re-engage in the lesson. No grudges! No resentment! As far as the misbehaving student is concerned their teacher has given them the power to control the situation and make the best choice (within certain respects). If the class time is nearing an end, I typically like to up the stakes and offer extra credit opportunities for my engaged participants. I continue to give the defiant learner clear shot opportunities to make up their class work at a later date during the intervention; however, my main objective is to encourage the student to re-evaluate their poor choice, and what it cost them, and to select a better choice the next time.

The defiant student might ponder on why the teacher is not feeding into their misbehavior. What if the teacher's tone and body language from the beginning establishes that there is no point to prove and no one to engage with, because everyone else is working (winning)? The student spends the class period trying to find a glitch in the system, while each moment ticks away, yet an open door for correction remains; it becomes a struggle of pride alone. The other students are participating (winning), the teacher is proud of their resiliency, even the teacher is winning, he/she appears content with my choice, but am I? I'm not hurting the teacher, the other kids are winning, I'm hurting myself...The teacher can reiterate this pattern to the student privately at a later time when it's time for the consequence of the misbehavior to be issued.

#9 Establish Leadership with Grace and Professionalism

Sometimes the student is able to take responsibility for their actions as they "simmer down" a bit. Other times, they cannot put the pieces together enough to see the error in their way. In either case they are choosing to be left behind in the class, ultimately in life. You can share this metaphor with the student privately. Your job is to ensure that they are aware of the consequences, and once they are you have to let them choose—that's life! You have to do your job for many years to come, and cannot become burned out by defiance alone. The student will observe you remaining in a peaceful state, while attempting to do the best you can to help them make better choices, yet the majority of your attention goes towards the positive learners who are appropriately engaged. I cannot tell you how affective this tactic has been for me as an educator!

- Incorporate moral lessons into the content or subject you are instructing soon after the behavior has occurred.

- Model what is expected of them in a calm, unmoved, yet with a directive demeanor.

- Share the effects of their choices with them privately as you consistently apply the consequence for their misbehavior.

Mystery Behaviors

As was stated earlier in this manual, students learn a lot from one another. They are their own worst critics and tend to be quite judgmental at any young age. They will rat on one another, and in great detail, when properly prompted to do so. Teachers are expected to know beforehand regarding every ongoing within their classroom, which is impossible. The good news is our students are more prone to spilling the beans if they feel compelled and comfortable to share. Trickery? Possibly. We have to utilize the resources around us, and who knows the matters of random ridiculousness that circulate the class/school more than the kids! The more you are informed, the more pro-active you can be as a lead alpha in your classroom.

Your goal is to categorize your students in levels of popularity, influence, age, gender, and strength. Please don't write this down! This is a mental note; we already do this anyways, but now you can see how beneficial this tactic can be in preventing a plethora of disruptions in your classroom, even your school. The kids are none the wiser, and you remain two steps ahead of the game. You'll talk casually to your students; ask questions while busying yourself with filing or grading. Invite some of your students to help you during breaks, establish an open-door policy, and allow them to see your fairness in all situations. You're almost too cool for school, and your students will tell you everything!

#10 You Will Not Save All of Your Students

You are not to interrogate the student(s) you've selected; rather to make them feel comfortable enough to talk. The kids will tell on each other, even kids who are gang affiliated leak. It is all about how you prompt them; you will get better at this with practice. You're not seeking to hurt them in any way, so be mindful of how you go about resolving informed matters once a trust is built. Like a classroom consigliore, they appreciate being able to share and vent to you, and they trust how you maintain a discrete resolution in all matters shared. By law, you are a mandated reporter, and in most cases you won't have to go to those extremes, so I highly suggest establishing this technique early on. Once they trust you, they will give you the scoop on matters throughout the school year that can assist you towards maintaining an effective learning environment!

The best teacher is a teacher who models what he/she expects from their pupils, one who rarely loses his/her cool, is often seen making strides to give students the best they have to give. That's our passion, that's why we teach! You will want to save them all! You will see that light within some that they don't see in themselves. No one is telling you to throw in the towel on a particular student(s); however, know in your heart of hearts that you will not save them all. Everyone has a mission while they're here on this earth, and yours is not to save every person that you encounter, neither is mine. Be okay with this notion, and do not use it as a reason to give up!

So that's it guys!! You might have noticed that we went over the 10,000 word mark, hopefully the information shared was worth the extra time spent, and it's all good. Being flexible is what makes us such great leaders, and now you can confidently rest assured that you don't have to be burned out in this line of work!

By developing a pro-active attitude about your position responsibilities, you will establish a structured learning environment that flows according to your divine gift of teaching. I pray that the information I have shared with you meets you in a good place in your educational career. That you have made a firm decision to be a teacher, and plan to ride the waves, good and bad, towards making a difference for every young person that you meet. You grabbed up this manual to get some straightforward advice on how to run a tight ship, and guarantee if you follow it you will! You're confident that you will grow strong, and build a bag of tricks that will amaze, enthuse, and inspire curiosity in your learners, and you will!

Now go out there and TEACH!

"Train up a child in the way he should go: and when he is old, he will not depart from it."

-Proverbs 22:6

Top 10 Creeds towards Becoming an Effective Educator

#1 Be Willing to Stay for the Long Haul

#2 Be Creatively Energetic

#3 Be Willing to Know & Learn your Kids

#4 Get Realistically Organized

#5 Address Negative Behaviors and be Consistent!

#6 A Lesson Planned is a Lesson Learned

#7 Document, Document, Document!

#8 Ask, and You Shall Receive Resources

#9 Establish Leadership with Grace & Professionalism

#10 You Will Not Save All of Your Students

Notes

Notes